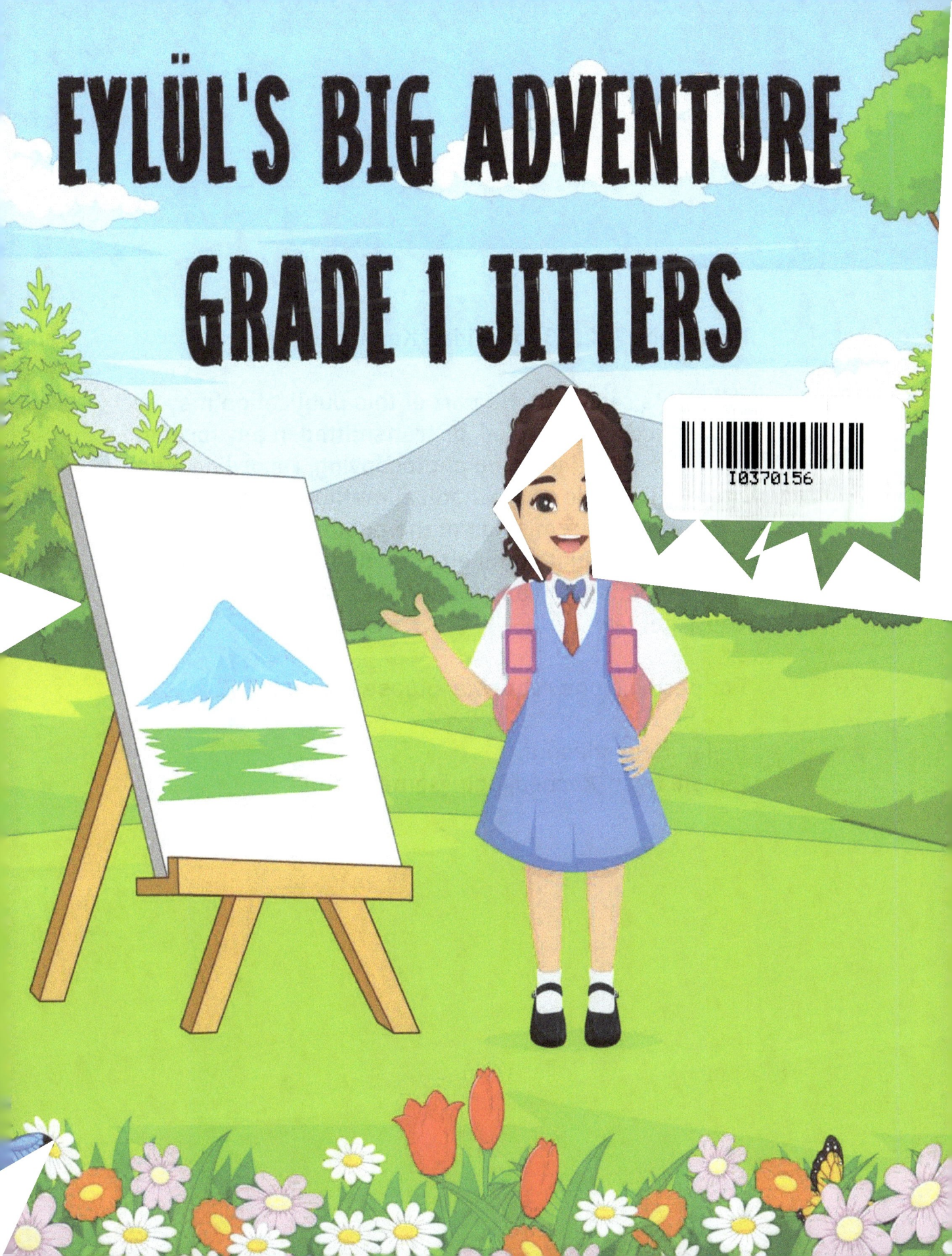

Copyright © [2023] by [Fidan Kechedjioglu]

All rights reserved. No part of this publication may be reproduced, distributed, or transmitted in any form or by any means, including photocopying, recording, or other electronic or mechanical methods, without the prior written permission of the publisher, except in the case of brief quotations embodied in critical reviews and certain other noncommercial uses permitted by copyright law.

For permissions requests, please contact:

[Fidan Kechedjioglu]
[Email: fidan_kechedjioglu@gmail.com]

Dedication Page:

For Eylül and All the Bright Stars Embarking on Grade One Adventures
In the magical world of education, where every day unfolds a new story, this book is dedicated to a special little girl named Eylül, whose journey into Grade 1 inspired these pages.

To Eylül, with her infectious laughter, and curls that dance like autumn leaves in the wind, may your days be filled with wonder, learning, and the joy of discovery. Your courage and resilience shine as brightly as the sun, guiding the way for others.

And to every young explorer stepping into the exciting world of Grade 1 from Kindergarten, this book is for you. May you find new friends, embrace challenges, and uncover the magic that lies within the pages of each day.

As you turn these pages, remember that you are not alone on this adventure. May your hearts be filled with curiosity, your minds with knowledge, and your days with the laughter of newfound friends.

Here's to a year of growth, fun, and countless stories waiting to be written!

With love and encouragement,
Fidan Kechedjioglu

Once upon a time, in a cozy town, lived a little girl named Eylül. She loved playing with her friends, exploring the park, and drawing colorful pictures. But one day, something big was about to happen – Eylül was going to start Grade 1!

As summer turned to fall, Eylül's excitement waned, replaced by nervous butterflies in her tummy. The thought of a new school, new teachers, and new friends made her feel a bit uneasy.

On the first day of school, Eylül put on her favorite shoes and carried her backpack filled with crayons and notebooks. She hesitated at the school gate, unsure about the unknown adventure waiting inside.

In her classroom, Eylül found a desk with her name on it. The teacher, Mrs. Meadows, welcomed her with a warm smile. Despite Mrs. Meadows' kindness, Eylül felt a bit lost in the sea of new faces.

Days passed, and Eylül started feeling a bit better. She made a friend named Lily, who liked drawing just as much as she did. Still, Grade 1 brought challenges – longer lessons, new subjects, and homework!

One day, Eylül decided to talk to Mrs. Meadows about her worries. Mrs. Meadows listened attentively and shared a secret with Eylül – even grown-ups feel nervous sometimes, especially when faced with something new.

Encouraged by this, Eylül embraced her Grade 1 adventure. She discovered that learning new things was exciting, and each day brought a chance to make more friends and share laughter.

As the school year continued, Eylül's jitters turned into joy. She found that Grade 1 wasn't as scary as she thought. Eylül learned, laughed, and even taught her classmates how to draw her favorite animals.

And so, Eylül's big adventure in Grade 1 became a story of overcoming worries, making friends, and discovering the magic of learning.

Meet Eylul:

Eylul, a lively six year old with a heart as big as her big curly brown hair, is the star of our story. Her infectious laughter make her a bundle of joy. Eylul loves drawing colourful pictures and exploring the world around her. As she embarks on the adventure of Grade 1, she discovers that courage comes in small packages, and her resilience lights up every page.
With a spirit as vibrant as her artwork, Eylul is a loveable character who reminds us all that even the smallest among us can have the biggest adventures.

Can you colour a picture of your first day of School?

www.ingramcontent.com/pod-product-compliance
Lightning Source LLC
Chambersburg PA
CBHW081238080526
44587CB00022B/3989